BUSES OF ACF
PHOTO ARCHIVE
INCLUDING ACF-BRILL AND CCF-BRILL

William A. Luke

Iconografix
Photo Archive Series

Iconografix
PO Box 446
Hudson, Wisconsin 54016 USA

© 2003 William A. Luke

All rights reserved. No part of this work may be reproduced or used in any form by any means... graphic, electronic, or mechanical, including photocopying, recording, taping, or any other information storage and retrieval system... without written permission of the publisher.

The information in this book is true and complete to the best of our knowledge. All recommendations are made without any guarantee on the part of the author or Publisher, who also disclaim any liability incurred in connection with the use of this data or specific details.

We acknowledge that certain words, such as model names and designations, mentioned herein are the property of the trademark holder. We use them for purposes of identification only. This is not an official publication.

Iconografix books are offered at a discount when sold in quantity for promotional use. Businesses or organizations seeking details should write to the Marketing Department, Iconografix, at the above address.

Library of Congress Card Number: 2003103541

ISBN 1-58388-101-8

03 04 05 06 07 08 09 5 4 3 2 1

Printed in China

Cover and book design by Dan Perry

Copyediting by Jane Mausser

COVER PHOTO: This ACF-Brill Model IC41 is the beautifully restored coach No. 1948 in the Greyhound Historic Bus Fleet. Originally it was owned by Southeastern Greyhound Lines, which took delivery of the bus in 1948. It was sold in 1954 and was owned by three persons until 1977 when the Greyhound Corporation bought it. Greyhound's Washington D. C. garage personnel restored the bus and it made its debut at the 1982 Knoxville World's Fair. (Thanks to Donald Coffin, bus historian, for the picture and the information.)

BOOK PROPOSALS

Iconografix is a publishing company specializing in books for transportation enthusiasts. We publish in a number of different areas, including Automobiles, Auto Racing, Buses, Construction Equipment, Emergency Equipment, Farming Equipment, Railroads & Trucks. The Iconografix imprint is constantly growing and expanding into new subject areas.

Authors, editors, and knowledgeable enthusiasts in the field of transportation history are invited to contact the Editorial Department at Iconografix, Inc., PO Box 446, Hudson, WI 54016.

Table of Contents

Acknowledgments 4
Introduction 5
Early ACF Intercity Buses 7
Early ACF City/Suburban Buses 20
ACF Model H-9 City Buses 25
ACF Model H-12 City Buses 27
ACF Model H-13 City Buses 29
ACF Model H-15 City Buses 32
ACF Model H-16 City Buses 35
ACF Model H-17 City Buses 38
ACF Model H-9 and H-15 Intercity Buses 42
ACF Model 25-U and 26-S City Buses 48
ACF Model 31-S City Buses 56
ACF Model 36-S City Buses 60
ACF Model 41-S and 45-S City Buses 62
ACF Model 37-P Intercity Buses 64
ACF Model 29-P Intercity Buses 70
ACF-Brill Model C-36 City/Suburban Buses 72
ACF-Brill Model C-44 City/Suburban Buses 76
ACF-Brill Model C-27 and C-31 City Buses 81
ACF-Brill IC-41 Intercity Buses 83
ACF-Brill C-10 Jitney Buses 92
ACF-Brill Trolley Buses 93
CCF-Brill IC-41 Intercity Buses 95
CCF-Brill Voyageur Intercity Buses 97
CCF-Brill Model IUC-35 Bus 99
CCF-Brill Model C-36 City Buses 100
CCF-Brill Model C-44A City Bus 102
CCF-Brill Model C-52 City Bus 103
CCF-Brill Trolley Buses 104
CanCar Model T-43 and T-52 City Buses 106
CCF-Brill Exported Buses 109
ACF and ACF-Brill Customer Time Tables 110
ACF and ACF-Brill Sales Literature 114
About the Author 126

Acknowledgments

Photographs in this book are from the bus history library of the author, William A. Luke, unless noted as photo credits from other individuals and organizations.

The following persons and organizations were very helpful in providing information that has made this book possible:

Donald Coffin, Bus Industry Historian, Hawley, Pennsylvania

Tom Jones, Librarian, Motor Bus Society, Clark, New Jersey

Paul Leger, President, Bus History Association, Halifax, Nova Scotia

Introduction

The abbreviation ACF represents American Car & Foundry Company, a pioneer transportation manufacturer. The company came into existence in 1899 as a result of the merger of 13 railroad-manufacturing companies, a very important industry at the time. The 19 American Car & Foundry Company factories not only produced new railroad cars, but also refurbished older cars.

Another transportation manufacturer, the J. G. Brill Corporation, built streetcars, interurban electric railcars, cars for steam railroads, and other railcars. The company also was involved in building buses, even assisting the Fifth Avenue Coach Co. of New York with some bus bodies.

The bus industry was emerging in the early 1920s at a rapid pace. The demand for buses, mainly for intercity services, was especially high. Cities were finding buses a less costly alternative to streetcars for certain routes.

In 1925, the bus-building business experienced a flurry of activity; in fact, the story became very long and complicated. When the dust cleared, The American Car & Foundry Company had control of the Brill Corporation. The Brill Corporation then controlled the American Car & Foundry Motors Company, Hall-Scott Motor Company, and Fageol Motors Company of Ohio. The J. G. Brill Company and the car-building companies it had acquired were also under the American Car & Foundry Company banner.

Although some bus bodies had been built before 1925, the new company began a bus-building program. A former railway car factory in Detroit was converted to build buses.

In the meantime, Frank and William Fageol, who had originally formed Fageol Motors of Ohio, sold to ACF. However, after a very short time, the Fageol brothers left ACF and acquired the Ohio plant, from which the revolutionary Twin Coach was introduced. This was partly the result of ACF's disinterest in the Fageols' ideas. Therefore, ACF went on without the Fageols and they actually competed with each other in bus building. The Twin Coach was far ahead of any model ACF was able to introduce.

At first, ACF built chassis for buses and various bus body builders would construct the body. However, ACF did build a number of complete buses. With Hall-Scott Motors as a part of the group, most buses produced by ACF were powered with Hall-Scott engines.

From the beginning, both intercity and transit buses were built by ACF. In 1931, the company decided to move the bus building from Detroit to Philadelphia, home of the Brill Organization.

It was there that a new series of buses was introduced with the Model designation H-9. It could have a body designed for city transit, and if so, the model had an "S" following H-9. If it had an intercity bus body design, it had a "P" designation. At this time, ACF decided to mount the engine under the floor of the bus for favorable weight distribution and other advantages. Almost every bus after that had an underfloor engine, and of course, the engine choice was one built by Hall-Scott Motors.

Between 1933 and 1937, several models featuring different sizes were introduced for city service. These were the H-12-S, H-13-S, H-15-S, and H-17-S. All had the underfloor Hall-Scott engines. Another series of city buses was launched in 1936: the 26-U, 26-S, 31-S, and 36-S models.

Intercity bus models were at first based on the H series, but in 1938 a new design was presented—first the 37-P, followed by the 29-P. ACF began to capture large orders for intercity buses, especially when the National Trailways Bus System was formed. Trailways companies made the ACF 37-P model and subsequent models their flagship buses. Southeastern Greyhound also became a good ACF customer for intercity buses. Large Hall-Scott engines were used, especially in the intercity buses. Air conditioning was also introduced in early intercity models.

World War II came and ACF production went into supplying products for the war effort. Some transit buses were supplied to the U.S. Navy in 1941.

After World War II, ACF—like most other bus manufacturers in the United States—brought out new intercity and transit bus models. At that time, the name for most models became ACF-Brill. In addition, trolley bus manufacturing and marketing came under the ACF-Brill name. However, trolley buses were manufactured in sizable numbers before World War II, but carried the Brill name. Bodies were similar to ACF bus bodies.

A total of 5,738 buses were built by ACF-Brill between 1945 and 1953. The most popular models were the C-36 city bus with 1,546 sold, and the IC-41 intercity model, with 1,375 units built.

Competition from General Motors, which had a very successful diesel engine, resulted in development of the bus most transit properties wanted. ACF-Brill could not compete, although a Cummins underfloor diesel engine was tried in the intercity buses. However, this competitive effort came too late, and in 1953, ACF-Brill exited the bus building business. City transit buses were unable to compete, and even trolley bus production ended.

Meanwhile, ACF-Brill had made an agreement with the Canadian Car & Foundry Company (CCF) following World War II. This agreement allowed the use of the ACF-Brill post-war design buses to be built in the CCF plant in Fort William (also known as Thunder Bay South), Ontario. Buses built by the company had the CCF-Brill name. The IC-41 intercity bus model was the first to be produced, and, by the end of 1952, approximately 1,300 units had been built.

The largest order for the CCF-Brill Model IC-41 was interesting. It came, in 1948, from the South African Railways. The 113 buses ordered had right-hand drive, as the rule of the road in South Africa is to the left.

CCF-Brill didn't stop building buses in 1953 as ACF-Brill did. Finding that diesel power for buses was more acceptable, CCF-Brill began offering transit buses to customers with British AEC 6-cylinder underfloor diesel engines.

In 1956, CCF-Brill adopted the name CanCar. Although bus production had virtually ended for CanCar in the mid-1950s, two new models were introduced in 1960: the TD-43 and the TD-51. Production lasted only three years, with 138 buses built.

CCF-Brill also produced trolley buses between 1945 and 1954. All were of the post-war design similar to the large transit buses. A total of 1,098 trolley buses were built by CCF-Brill. In 1945, three Canadian cities were operating trolley buses. Twelve more decided to operate trolley buses following World War II, which gave CCF-Brill a big market for a few years.

ACF and ACF-Brill buses had an important place in the history of bus transportation in the United States, and CCF-Brill had a prominent role in Canadian bus transportation history.

Early ACF Intercity Buses

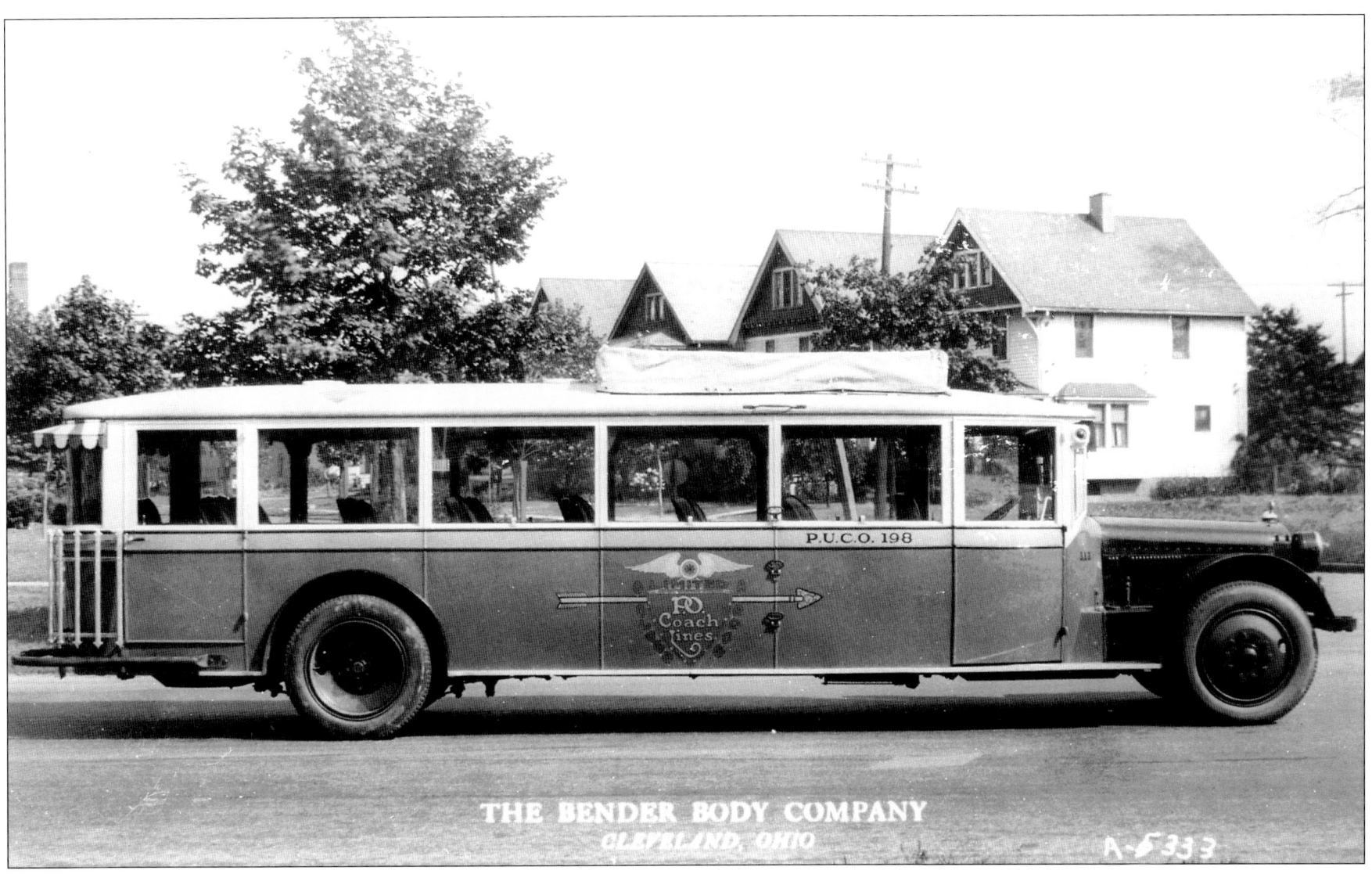

Penn Ohio Coach Lines of Youngstown, Ohio, operated one of the first ACF intercity buses. Bender Body Company of Cleveland, Ohio, built the body. In the early days, ACF buses involved the chassis only, with various body builders chosen by the operators to supply the bodies. This Penn Ohio bus joined the fleet in 1925. The company originated in 1922. *Don Coffin Collection*

These two ACF Model 508-2 B-3 buses went into service in 1927 for Union Pacific Stages. That was the same year the Union Pacific Railroad decided to operate bus service, and the Union Pacific Stages company was incorporated. It initially operated buses between Portland and Pendleton, Oregon, but service was later extended into Washington and Idaho. The Model 508-2 B-3 bus seated 29 passengers and had a Hall-Scott 110-horsepower 468-cubic-inch engine. *Don Coffin Collection*

The Yelloway System was the name used by a number of bus companies to cooperatively operate a sizable long-distance route service between California and the Midwest. In 1927, this ACF Model 508-2 B-3 operated under the Yelloway name. The belt line of the bus indicated several of the cities served. The bus also had a large canvas enclosed baggage rack on the roof. The Yelloway system joined with Pioneer Stages in 1928 and later that year merged into the new Greyhound. *Don Coffin Collection*

Eastern Michigan Motorbuses of Detroit originated in 1928, succeeding Peoples Motor Coach Company, a subsidiary of the Detroit United Railways. In 1929, Eastern Michigan Motorbuses consisted of suburban bus lines in the Detroit area, but there was also a longer route linking Detroit with Grand Rapids and Lansing, Michigan. *Don Coffin Collection*

One of Missouri Pacific Transportation Company's first buses was this ACF Model 602-1 bus purchased in 1929, a year after the company began. The bus accommodated 23 passengers and had a body built by Lang Body Co. of Cleveland, Ohio. Missouri Pacific Transportation was originally headquartered in Little Rock, Arkansas. Most of the original routes were acquired by purchasing small bus companies in Arkansas and South Texas. *Don Coffin Collection*

ACF built chassis for many buses that had bodies built by various bus-body builders. Such was the case with this 1932 Model 508-3 B-3 ACF. It had a deck-and-a-half body built by Heiser Body Co. of Seattle, Washington. The design was very popular on the West Coast with companies such as North Coast Line because it offered increased baggage space and greater passenger visibility on the upper level. North Coast Lines operated this bus. The company operated service between Portland, Oregon, and Vancouver, British Columbia, via Seattle. *Don Coffin Collection*

Southland Greyhound Lines of Fort Worth, Texas, referred to its western services as the West Texas Division following the acquisition of West Texas Coaches in September 1929. That same year, Southland bought two ACF Model 160-230-P30 buses and assigned them to the West Texas Division. Hall-Scott Model 160 468-cubic-inch engines were mounted at the front of these buses. Very few of this type ACF bus were built.

Service Stages of Anniston, Alabama, acquired this ACF Model 602-IB3 in March 1930. It was reported that it was one of the last ACF buses built with a Model 612 chassis. Service Stages operated an important route between Birmingham, Alabama, and Atlanta, Georgia, which was later taken over by Southeastern Greyhound Lines. *Motor Bus Society*

John A. Towns of Harrisonville, Virginia, purchased 12 of these ACF Model P-216 buses for his Shenandoah Stages bus operation in Virginia. The route was through a number of cities in the Shenandoah Valley. The rear of these buses had grillework, and baggage could be accommodated on the rear roof of the bus. This model was one of the few buses built by ACF that did not have a Hall-Scott engine; a Hercules WXC-3 engine was used. *Motor Bus Society*

This ACF Model 901-1-P64 was purchased by Michigan's Owosso-Flint Bus Lines in 1931. The Model 901-1-P64 ACF was built in Detroit, and most were acquired in small numbers by intercity bus companies. This model had a 175-horsepower 707-cubic-inch Hall-Scott engine. Owosso-Flint Bus Line, an early pioneer bus company founded in 1913, operated under the name Indian Trails. The main route was between Flint, Michigan, and Chicago; this is the same route operated by the company today, but due to expansion, other routes are also being operated.

The Bee Line, Rockville Center, New York, purchased a number of ACF buses from 1927 through 1932, and again in 1939. This bus and 37 others were purchased in 1931–1932. The Bee Line began in 1922 with a 3-mile route and expanded with a number of routes in the New York City suburban area. It also was involved in charter and tour business. In 1937, Bee Line had 111 buses, approximately three-fourths of which were ACFs.

Cayuga Omnibus Corporation of Auburn, New York, bought five ACF Model P-30 29-passenger buses in June 1930. They had 468-cubic-inch Hall-Scott Model 160 engines. Cayuga Omnibus began in 1927 with a city service in Auburn plus an intercity service of 25 miles between Auburn and Syracuse, New York. City service ended in 1949, and the intercity route was sold to Onondaga Coach Corporation in 1953. *Motor Bus Society*

Frank Martz Coach Lines of Wilkes-Barre, Pennsylvania, purchased five of these ACF Model 801-1-P-45A buses with Bender Body Company bodies in October 1930. Frank Martz Coach began in 1912 as White Transit Company, primarily because Martz was a White Motor Company distributor. Some of the early White buses had Brill bodies. The first services of the company were local routes, but in 1927, the name Frank Martz Coach Company was adopted and intercity service began. At one time Martz buses operated between Chicago and New York City. *Don Coffin Collection*

Early ACF City/Suburban Buses

The only double-deck buses built by ACF were 50 Model 519-4-F1 gas-electric vehicles. They were delivered beginning in November 1926 for the Detroit Street Railway Company. The buses accommodated 60 passengers and used Hall-Scott 110-horsepower 468-cubic-inch engines. *Motor Bus Society*

This city bus with innovative standee windows was one of the first ACF buses built. This prototype was shown to the bus industry, but it did not create interest. It was built in the ACF plant in Kent, Ohio, before the plant's acquisition by the Fageol brothers. ACF moved bus production to Detroit soon afterward. *Motor Bus Society*

When Public Service of New Jersey replaced streetcar lines of Morris County Traction Company in 1928, 38 ACF Model 508-6-D14 buses—one of which is pictured here—were substituted. The 8,900-pound buses had Hall-Scott Model 110 468-cubic-inch engines mounted in the front. *Motor Bus Society*

The Metropolitan ACF Model H-10 bus was introduced in 1928 as an attempt to compete with the dual-engined Twin Coach. Approximately 325 were built until 1931, when the model was discontinued. The Boston Elevated Railway had 110 of these buses in its fleet and the Detroit Street Railway acquired 94, one of which is pictured here. *Motor Bus Society*

In May 1930, Public Service Coordinated Transport operated several divisions in New Jersey and at the time 20 ACF Model 700-1-P40 buses were bought. These were deluxe intercity models, but with transit-type leaf doors. They were used to replace some streetcar lines of the Morris County Traction Company, which had just been acquired. It was reported that 38 buses were built by ACF with the 701 chassis. *Motor Bus Society*

ACF Model H-9 City Buses

A total of 354 Model H-9 ACF buses were built in the Philadelphia plant, with the first produced in 1933. The Boston Elevated Railway owned 128 of the Model H-9 ACF; it acquired the bus pictured in 1937. The Boston transit operator bought its first ACF bus, a Model 519-5-D-10, in 1927, and had 114 ACF Detroit-built buses before 1933.

The Model H-9-S ACF bus, the first ACF to have an underfloor engine, was introduced in 1934. ACF engineers felt the underfloor position of the Hall-Scott 180-horsepower engine would provide good weight distribution and other advantages. The first company to order the new bus was the Eastern Massachusetts Street Railway Company of Boston. Initially, 5 were delivered, followed by another 43 late in 1934. Eastern Massachusetts received four more Model H-9-S ACF buses as late as 1941. Eastern Massachusetts Street Railway Company was a good ACF customer; it purchased most of the manufacturer's pre-World War II models.

ACF Model H-12 City Buses

Staten Island Coach Co. of New York City purchased 13 ACF Model H-12-S buses in early 1934. Later that year and in 1935 and 1936, the company purchased 41 more units of this model. The H-12-S had certain style changes but retained its 22-passenger size. Staten Island Coach Co. originated in the mid-1920s, but did not become a participant in bus routes on the island until 1933. In 1946, the company elected not to renew its franchise, and Isle Transportation Co. took over. *Motor Bus Society*

This ACF Model H-12-S bus was one of the last of 242 of this model built beginning in 1933. Chicago & Calumet District Transit Company of Hammond, Indiana, took delivery of this bus and 11 others in July 1934. The Chicago & Calumet District Transit Company used the name "Shore Line" because of its operation along the Lake Michigan shore between Indiana communities and downtown Chicago.

28

ACF Model H-13 City Buses

Scranton Transit in Pennsylvania bought three ACF Model H-13-S buses in 1936–1937 to operate a new suburban route. Following this purchase, Scranton added four Model 26-S and one Model 31-S ACF buses. The first buses reported to have operated in 1923 were by a subsidiary of the streetcar company. The ACF Model H-13-S buses like the ones in Scranton had Hall-Scott Model 130 underfloor engines.

This Model H-13-S ACF bus was one of the five purchased by the Southern Pennsylvania Bus Company of Chester, Pennsylvania, in early 1937. This is an interesting left rear view of the bus, showing the spare tire mounted at the rear and the small emergency door. Southern Pennsylvania Bus Company had its start in the mid-1920s, serving the city of Chester and a number of neighboring communities. The company was sold to Philadelphia Suburban Transportation Company in 1960.

Several independent bus associations have operated in New Jersey including the South Hudson County Bus Owners Association. Member companies operated their buses on the street between Jersey City and Bayonne. The association had 67 individual owners; each was assigned a bus number preceded with a "B." Therefore, bus B-53, an ACF Model H-13-S, was owned by Frank Duprey's FD&DS Bus Company, located in Bayonne. It was acquired in 1938. Most Model H-13-S ACF buses had two doors for city operation but this one only had one door.

ACF Model H-15 City Buses

This is an unusual picture of an ACF Model H-15-S bus, taken at the ACF factory in Philadelphia in 1938. It had been ordered by the New Britain Transportation Company of Connecticut, but the order was cancelled before it was to be delivered. The Cumberland and Westernport Transit Company in Frostburg, Maryland, reportedly acquired the bus. A total of 191 Model H-15-S ACF buses were built.

Late in 1934, ACF introduced the Model H-15-S bus. The first company to order this new 29-passenger city bus was Triple Cities Traction Company of Binghamton, New York, which took delivery of seven units in February 1935. Three more were added in 1937. Streetcars, which began serving the area in the 1880s, were discontinued in 1930 when Triple Cities began replacing the streetcars with buses. The name Triple Cities refers to Binghamton, Endicott, and Johnson City. *Motor Bus Society*

Plymouth & Brockton Street Railway Company in Massachusetts was one of many New England bus companies that operated ACF buses. This Model H-15-S ACF is one of the company's buses. The Plymouth & Brockton Street Railway Company was a pioneer in operating transportation service, beginning with a Plymouth-Kingston streetcar line in 1889. Streetcars were operated until 1928 when buses assumed all services. The Plymouth & Brockton Street Railway Company continues to operate today, with a fleet of 66 buses.

ACF Model H-16 City Buses

Eastern Massachusetts Street Railway Company of Boston was one of ACF's best customers. The ACF Model H-16-S, a 42-passenger bus pictured here, was part of a 10-bus order in June 1936. The Model H-16-S was the largest H series city bus built by ACF. Eastern Massachusetts purchased 68 additional ACF Model H-16-S buses, including the last order for this model in 1941. The company served a large suburban area of Boston. In 1937, the company had more than 500 buses; more than half were built by ACF. *Motor Bus Society*

In the two-door configuration, the ACF Model H-16-S bus had seats for 42 passengers. The Model H-16-S had a Hall-Scott 180-horsepower gasoline engine mounted under the bus floor. ACF built 320 of this model between 1935 and 1941. *Motor Bus Society*

Most of the ACF Model H-16-S buses were purchased by large urban bus operators in the East. Houston Electric Company was the only exception. It had 24 of the Model H-16-S buses, one of which is pictured here. Houston Electric began operating buses in 1924. In the early 1940s, streetcars were abandoned and Houston became an all-bus city. The company had a highly mixed fleet. *Motor Bus Society*

ACF Model H-17 City Buses

The Evanston and Niles Center Bus Company in Illinois began in 1929, and eight years later merged with the Evanston Railway Company to become Evanston Bus Company. The Evanston and Niles Center Bus Company had only 24 buses; half the fleet was ACF buses including this Model H-17-S bus, which was acquired in 1936 with three others. These buses seated 35 passengers and had a 183-1/2-inch wheelbase.

This ACF Model H-17-S bus was a single purchase by the New North State Railways for service in Utica, New York, in 1938. It was the only Model H-17-S in the mixed Utica fleet, although four Model H-12-S ACF buses saw service in Utica. ACF built 551 Model H-17-S buses between 1935 and 1938.

ACF's 35-passenger Model H-17-S was first presented in 1935. It proved to be one of the most popular ACF buses in the pre-World War II era. Many transit systems like the Pennsylvania's Harrisburg Railways Company bought the Model H-17-S ACF. In 1935, Harrisburg purchased 20 units like the one shown. Harrisburg Railways also had 12 Model H-12-S and 27 H-15-S ACF buses.

Boston, Worcester & New York Street Railway Company of Framingham, Massachusetts, was one of many New England bus companies that used ACF buses. It had eight Model H-15-S ACF buses and one Model H-17-S. The H-17-S was the last of that model built, and was purchased by the company in December 1938. Boston, Worcester & New York Street Railway Company operated a main route between Boston and Worcester. It also had considerable suburban service and was commonly known as the B & W Lines. At one time, the company operated streetcars, but they were eliminated in 1932.

ACF Model H-9 and H-15 Intercity Buses

In June 1935, Southeastern Greyhound Lines of Lexington, Kentucky, bought five ACF Model H-9-P buses. This was the company's first ACF order, and one of the first Model H-9-P units built for an intercity bus company. These buses were the first of many Southeastern Greyhound Lines bought from ACF between 1935 and 1948. The Model H-9-P intercity bus had a Hall-Scott 180-horsepower engine mounted under the floor. *Don Coffin Collection*

The Model H-9 ACF was available in both city and intercity versions. City transit companies ordered most of the first H-9 ACF buses. By 1935, intercity companies including Quaker Transportation Company of Philadelphia became interested in the Model H-9 ACF. In 1937 and 1938, Quaker purchased three of these models including a demonstrator. Quaker operated half-hour daytime service and hourly evening service between Philadelphia and New York City.

The Atchison, Topeka & Santa Fe Railway acquired two ACF Model H-15-S transit buses late in 1936. The buses had front entrance/exit doors on both sides. This two-door arrangement was built into these buses so they could be used for passengers transferring to and from train side. The railway company also had two Model H-9-S ACF buses.

The Norfolk Southern Bus Company in Virginia, a subsidiary of the Norfolk Southern Railway, was one of a number of railroad-owned intercity bus operations. The Norfolk Southern Bus Company began in 1926 with a Norfolk-Virginia Beach bus service. The ACF Model H-9-P pictured here was purchased in 1937, and was one of four H-9-P buses in the fleet. Between 1933 and 1941, 177 intercity Model H-9-P ACF buses were built.

Campus Coach Lines of New York City was just getting its start when this ACF Model H-9-P coach was acquired in 1938. Another ACF Model H-9-P bus was purchased a year later. Campus Coach Lines, operated by Campus Travel, Inc. specialized in charter services. The Model H-9-P buses had Hall-Scott Model 180 707-cubic-inch engines.

Southeastern Greyhound Lines of Lexington, Kentucky, and its subsidiary, Union Bus Company, bought three ACF Model H-15-P 28-passenger buses in December 1937. ACF built a number of H-15-S buses for city services, but only 25 were built as intercity buses. Normally, the Model H-9-P had square side windows, but these Southeastern Greyhound Model H-15-P buses had rounded-corner windows. *Don Coffin Collection*

47

ACF Model 25-U and 26-S City Buses

The ACF Model 26-U, first introduced in 1938, had a Hall-Scott Model 95 engine mounted under the floor. The Model 26-U was similar to the ACF Model 26-S, except the front wheels were located ahead of the entrance/exit door. It had limited production, with only 50 units built in four years.

The Jersey City and Montclair Bus Co. bought four ACF Model 26-U buses in 1939. The buses were used on a route that connected with the Hudson and Manhattan Railroad Company trains from New Jersey to and from New York City. This Model 26-U had high-back seats. Only 50 of these small buses were built.

Rochester Transit Corporation in New York bought five ACF Model 26-S buses in November 1939. These buses had an interesting rooftop ventilating system. The small Model 26-S bus had a Hall-Scott Model 95 engine mounted under the floor. Two hundred were built between 1938 and 1942.

Oahu Railway and Land Company, which began as a steam railroad service in 1889, was one of the small rural transportation companies on Hawaii's island of Oahu. Bus service was operated in the 1930s with 10 small ACF Model 26-S buses (one pictured here), 2 acquired in 1938, and 8 more in 1941. These buses had high-back seats. Oahu Railway and Land was probably ACF's most distant customer.

In 1933, ACF began positioning its buses' engines horizontally under the floor. For 20 years, starting in the mid-1930s, all ACF-Brill and ACF-produced buses had underfloor engines. Hall-Scott Motors provided engines of several sizes. Pictured here is the underside of a Model 26-S ACF bus, showing the location of the Hall-Scott Model HS-95 gasoline engine. *Motor Bus Society*

Alexandria, Bancroft & Washington Transit Company—better known as AB&W Transit—was formed in late 1934, although its roots date back to the nineteenth century as an electric railway. It was headquartered in Alexandria, Virginia, across the Potomac River from Washington, D.C. In 1938 and 1939, AB&W Transit purchased 20 of these ACF Model 26-S buses.

The Biddeford and Saco Street Railway Company of Saco, Maine, began in 1887 with streetcars serving a small area in southern Maine. Buses replaced the streetcars in 1939 and the company later became known as the Biddeford and Saco Bus Company. It went out of business in 1979 when a public agency took over the bus service. This ACF Model 26-S, the sixth in the company's fleet, was a single-bus purchase in July 1940.

Conestoga Transportation Company of Lancaster, Pennsylvania, bought mostly ACF or ACF-Brill city buses between 1935 and 1949. In 1940, 10 ACF Model 26-S buses were added to 6 of the same model acquired in an earlier delivery. A Hall-Scott 95-horsepower 377-cubic-inch underfloor engine powered the bus.

ACF Model 31-S City Buses

Chicago & West Towns Railways, Inc. of Oak Park, Illinois, which operated streetcars for many years, began its first bus route in 1931. The system served a number of Cook County suburbs just west of Chicago. Five of these bright blue-and-cream Model 31-S ACF buses were acquired in 1940. The Model 31-S had the Hall-Scott Model 130 engine. Between 1939 and 1942, 425 Model 31-S units were built.

Penobscot Transportation Company, a subsidiary of the Bangor Hydro Company in Maine, was formed April 29, 1940. Penobscot Transportation began bus service in the Bangor area when the first streetcar line was replaced by buses. Remaining streetcar lines ended in 1945, leaving only buses serving the area. This ACF Model 31-S bus entered the Penobscot fleet in early 1941. Two were delivered earlier and within two years, the property had 14 Model 31-S ACFs. Penobscot Transportation was sold to Range Transportation Company in January 1951.

Virginia's Roanoke Railway and Electric Company, which had the local streetcar system, first operated buses in 1924. Although buses carried the Roanoke Railway and Electric Company name, they were operated by Safety Motor Transit, a subsidiary formed in 1928. The only ACF buses to operate in the Roanoke area were 18 ACF Model 31-S buses (one shown here), ordered in 1940 and 1941.

The Middlesex and Boston Street Railway Company of Waltham, Massachusetts, bought five of the first ACF 31-S buses (one pictured here) in September 1939. These buses had one door and lower window bars. The company operated a number of routes with service as frequent as 20–30 minutes in the suburban area west of Boston. Middlesex and Boston Street Railway originally had streetcars when it began in 1905, but buses had replaced all the streetcars by 1931. The Massachusetts Bay Transportation Authority acquired the company in 1972.

ACF Model 36-S City Buses

This ACF Model 36-S was the last of 20 of this model acquired by the United Electric Railway of Providence, Rhode Island, in 1939 and 1940. The Model 36-S was one of ACF's most popular city buses with 551 reportedly built between 1938 and 1942.

Montreal, Quebec, was the only Canadian city to acquire ACF buses. This Model 36-S was one of 10 that went to the Montreal Tramways Company in 1939. Ten more were added in 1941. Other ACF buses that saw service in Montreal were 20 Model H-13-S buses and 8 Model 26-S units. Montreal operated a variety of bus makes, although not a large fleet compared to other cities because of the predominance of streetcars serving the city.

61

ACF Model 41-S and 45-S City Buses

The ACF-Brill Model 41-S bus was introduced in 1941, and 191 units were built in three years. Aronimik Transportation Company, also known as the Red Arrow Lines of Upper Darby, Pennsylvania, operated 10 ACF 41-S buses delivered in December 1941. Red Arrow Lines was a subsidiary of the Philadelphia and West Chester Traction Company, serving the Philadelphia suburban area primarily from the 69th Street Terminal. The company began in 1923 and was acquired by the Southeastern Pennsylvania Transit Authority in 1970. *Motor Bus Society*

The ACF Model 45-S—the largest pre-World War II ACF city bus—was introduced in 1941, but only 51 units were built due to wartime restrictions on supplies. This model had a 194-horsepower Hall-Scott underfloor engine, and an overall length of 34 feet, 10-1/2 inches. Triboro Coach Corporation of Jackson Heights, New York, bought 24 of these buses, one of which is pictured here. Triboro, a prominent transit carrier in the New York City borough of Queens, was incorporated in 1931 and continues to operate today. *Motor Bus Society*

ACF Model 37-P Intercity Buses

Carolina Coach Company of Raleigh, North Carolina, began in 1925, the same year it made its first purchase of ACF buses. When ACF introduced the 37-P intercity coach in 1938, Carolina initially bought four for its fleet. Two more followed later that year, and three in 1939. Carolina Coach used the 37-passenger Model 37-P ACF buses on its main line route between Richmond and Norfolk, Virginia, and Atlanta, Georgia. ACF built 209 Model 37-P coaches.

One of the interesting ACF Model 37-P buses was this one used by the U.S. Military Academy in West Point, New York. Avery's Garage in Highland Falls, New York, took delivery of this coach and one other in September 1939. This Model 37-P had a Model 180 707-cubic-inch Hall-Scott gasoline engine mounted under the floor.

The Model 37-P ACF intercity coach was very popular. Several variations of the model were built between 1938 and 1942. Boston and Maine Transportation Company, a subsidiary of the Boston and Maine Railroad, had 10 of these coaches; the first was delivered in June 1938, with the remainder a year later. Boston and Maine Transportation began in 1927 with routes from Boston to cities in Maine and New Hampshire. The company joined the National Trailways Bus System in 1952. Greyhound Lines bought the bus routes in 1957. *Paul Leger Collection*

One of Pennsylvania's oldest bus companies was Edwards Transit Company of Williamsport, incorporated in 1921. Because it connected New York City with Cleveland on Lake Erie, the company became known as Edwards Lakes-to-Sea-Stages. Two ACF Model 37-PB coaches were acquired in 1941 and early 1942 (No. 119 pictured here). Five ACF coaches were already in the fleet. The Model 37-PB ACF had a Model 180 Hall-Scott underfloor engine.

Blue Ridge Lines of Hagerstown, Maryland, was an important intercity bus company with a major route from Washington and Baltimore to and from Pittsburgh before World War II. In 1940, Blue Ridge purchased its first ACF buses: 25 Model 27-PB buses and 5 Model 37-PBS ACF units. The ACF 37-PB pictured here had silver siding added at the Blue Ridge shop in 1950 to give it a more modern look. Blue Ridge sold its intercity routes to Greyhound in 1955. *Don Coffin Collection*

Florida Motor Lines was the important intercity bus company in Florida from its inception in 1914 until 1946, when Greyhound Lines acquired the company. In 1936, Florida Motor Lines bought it first ACF buses, which were H-9-P models. The ACF Model 37-P pictured here was the next ACF model acquired. Seven of these were added to the fleet in 1938. Further orders involving ACF Models 37-P, 37-PB, and 37-PBS came in 1939 through 1942. Florida Motor Lines operated 51 ACF buses, most of which were air-conditioned.

ACF Model 29-P Intercity Buses

Texas Motorcoaches, Inc. of Fort Worth became the owner of one of the first Model 29-P ACF coaches. The Model 29-P pictured is one of 10 units delivered on August 29, 1940. This Model 29-P was in a new series of ACF intercity coaches. It had 29 seats and an underfloor Hall-Scott Model 135 engine. Texas Motorcoaches was operating half-hour daytime schedules between Fort Worth and Dallas.

After a few early months in 1940, ACF modified the Model 29-PB with vertically opening side windows. The innovative seating had space below each seat for baggage. Interurban Transportation of Alexandria, Louisiana, took delivery of 10 Model 29-PB coaches in 1941. Interurban, which had just joined the National Trailways Bus System, also took delivery of six ACF Model 37-PB buses in 1941.

ACF-Brill Model C-36 City/Suburban Buses

The Springfield Street Railway Company in Massachusetts began running buses in 1924. Until 1950, the company operated three different makes of buses including ACF. The first ACFs in the fleet were three Model H-17-S buses. Then came 12 Model 26-S ACF buses in 1940. In 1947 and 1948, the company acquired 40 ACF-Brill Model C-36 buses, one of which is pictured here. In 1974, the public Pioneer Valley Transit Authority took over the Springfield Street Railway Company.

After World War II, Houston Electric Company continued to have a mixed fleet including ACF-Brill Model C-36 buses. In June 1946, Houston Electric purchased 10 of the first Model C-36 ACF-Brills. More were added in the next year, making 56 in the Houston fleet. After 1947, Houston Electric standardized with General Motors buses.

The Des Moines Railway Co. had eight ACF-Brill Model C-36 buses (one pictured here). Although Des Moines only had a small bus fleet, it had a large trolley bus fleet. Following World War II, the Des Moines Railway Co. acquired 85 ACF-Brill Model TC-44 and T-46 trolley buses. It had begun its trolley bus system in 1938.

Like many New England bus companies large and small, Interstate Transit Corporation, a small bus company headquartered in Attleboro, Massachusetts, had ACF and ACF-Brill buses in its fleet. It purchased five of these ACF-Brill Model C-36 buses in 1947. The company, originally known as Interstate Street Railway Company, began operating buses in 1924 and had its first ACF bus in 1928. Service was primarily between Attleboro, Pawtucket, and Providence, Rhode Island.

ACF-Brill Model C-44 City/Suburban Buses

Chicago Surface Lines operated many buses from a number of manufacturers. ACF and ACF-Brill buses were part of the fleet. The first ACF buses came in 1934. After World War II, 133 Model C-36 and 106 Model C-44 ACF-Brill buses were ordered. The Model C-44 (one pictured here) was the largest ACF-Brill transit bus built. It had a 180-horsepower 707-cubic-inch Hall-Scott underfloor engine.

Although Philadelphia was the home of ACF and ACF-Brill, the transit systems in Philadelphia did not purchase many buses from the hometown builder. In 1947, the first order of 85 Model C-44 ACF-Brill buses (one pictured here) went to the Philadelphia Transportation Company. These were the only post World War II ACF-Brill buses for Philadelphia. However, in 1939 and the early 1940s, Philadelphia Rapid Transit had 158 Model 31-S ACF buses.

Public Service Interstate Transportation Company of Newark, New Jersey, bought 17 ACF-Brill Model C-44 suburban buses in November 1947. These buses, which seated 45 passengers, were the only ACF-Brill buses operated by Public Service, as General Motors dominated the company's bus fleet.

Continental Bus System of Dallas was an important nationwide intercity bus company. In addition to long-distance services, Continental operated some suburban bus services, particularly in the Dallas and Kansas City areas. The company purchased six Model C-44 ACF-Brill buses for its suburban services in August 1947. One is pictured here leaving the Dallas Interurban Station. The Model C-44 was the largest ACF-Brill transit bus at the time; 1,089 of this model were built.

One of the last orders for the ACF-Brill Model C-44 was for 16 units for the Atomic Energy Commission for the National Reactor Testing Station in Arco, a small central Idaho community. In 1950, this site was established for the reactor, which five years later supplied electrical power to Arco, the first community in the world to have all its power generated by nuclear energy. A large fleet of buses brought workers to and from Arco and Pocatello, Idaho Falls, and other locations. Earlier, 20 similar ACF-Brill Model C-44s were delivered to the Atomic Energy Commission. Note the bus pictured has a sedan-type door, not typical on the C-44 Model.

ACF-Brill Model C-27 and C-31 City Buses

In 1948, ACF-Brill announced two new small bus models, the Model C-27 (shown here) and the C-31. These buses had a design similar to the larger ACF-Brill post-World War II transit buses. Instead of having Hall-Scott engines, which powered almost all previous ACF and ACF-Brill buses, the new small buses had International 6-cylinder 361-cubic-inch gasoline engines. International 269-cubic-inch or 401-cubic-inch engines were optional.

Pioneer Bus Company of Houston was one of several suburban bus companies in the rapidly growing Houston area. Pioneer bought this Brill C-31 and had 15 others in 1951. They were the only Brills in the Pioneer fleet. Pioneer Bus Company began in 1936 and was sold in 1964 to Rapid Transit Lines, the operator of Houston bus services at that time.

ACF-Brill IC-41 Intercity Buses

The first ACF-Brill Model IC-41 intercity coaches were ordered by Vermont Transit Co. of Burlington, and were delivered in December 1945. A year later, Vermont Transit bought six more of this model. The Model IC-41 had a Hall-Scott 190-2 underfloor 779-cubic-inch gasoline engine. The first Model IC-41 coaches were distinguished by a small grille in the front.

Santa Fe Trail Transportation Co. of Wichita, Kansas, was the largest user of ACF and ACF-Brill intercity coaches between 1936 and 1947. ACF Model H-9-P coaches were the first purchased by Santa Fe in 1936, and some of these were the first to have air conditioning. The company began in 1933, and in 1936 became a founding member of the National Trailways Bus System. This Model IC-41 ACF-Brill coach was one of the first of 152 of this model bought by Santa Fe in 1946 and 1947. In 1947, Santa Fe became a part of the Transcontinental Bus System (Continental Trailways).

ACF-Brill made a minor style change in the Model IC-41 coach in 1947, with four chrome strips over the front grille and lowered headlights. Ohio Greyhound Lines took delivery of 122 of these Model IC-41 coaches in January 1947. Although most Greyhound companies bought General Motors coaches, some had ACF-Brill coaches. Southeastern Greyhound Lines was an exception; its fleet had almost all ACF and ACF-Brill coaches from 1937 until 1952.

ACF-Brill made another styling change to the Model IC-41 coaches in early 1948. The four chrome stripes across the front were extended to almost the entire lower front area. Fluted aluminum sides were also an option. Chicago's American Bus Lines chose this option for some of its coaches, including this one delivered in March 1948 with nine others. American Bus Lines had 87 ACF-Brill Model IC-41 coaches in its fleet.

Maine Central Transportation Company of Portland, a subsidiary of Maine Central Railroad, bought six of these ACF-Brill Model IC 37/41 coaches in December 1946. The bus routes were originally under the SamOset Company name. That company operated short bus routes to and from hotels it served, beginning in 1925. The Maine Central Transportation Company originated in 1932 and assumed the SamOset bus routes in addition to pioneering longer routes in Maine.

A new ACF-Brill Model IC-41A was introduced in September 1951. There were some minor styling changes. The grille in the front was eliminated, the windshields were channeled in rubber, and new aluminum siding was added to create a new look for the coach. A new air-conditioning system driven from the Hall-Scott Model 190-5 gasoline engine was another improvement. In March 1952, the Cummins Diesel NHHB-600 4-cycle diesel engine was made available for the Model IC-41AD (the D was added for diesel).

The driver's area of the ACF-Brill IC-41 is shown here. The driver was seated over the left front wheel, and to the right was seating for two passengers. The entrance/exit door was behind the front wheel. Automatic transmission had not become standard or even an option in 1951 when this ACF-Brill coach was announced. It had a Spicer four-speed manual transmission.

The ACF-Brill Model IC-41A coach seated 41 passengers in reclining seats. Each seat had space below for baggage and overhead racks. The underfloor engine limited the amount of space in underfloor compartments, but a large compartment in the rear was also available.

This one-of-a-kind, deck-and-a-half design was adapted from a normal Model IC-37/41 ACF-Brill coach beginning in 1947. It was specially built for Continental Trailways, which had plans to have 450 of these coaches. This particular experimental coach saw service for Continental in several areas of the country before it was retired. It was powered by a 267-horsepower Hall-Scott gasoline engine mounted underfloor.

ACF-Brill C-10 Jitney Buses

One of the unusual ACF-Brill buses was a small jitney, designated the Model C-10. It was built in 1948 in cooperation with Arthur Motors, Inc. of Atlantic City, New Jersey. That company supplied the Willys truck chassis and ACF-Brill built the bodies. The jitney service in Atlantic City operated 25 of these buses on Pacific Avenue. One of the C-10 ACF-Brills is shown here. *Motor Bus Society*

ACF-Brill Trolley Buses

Trolley buses were built in the ACF Philadelphia plant. They had similar styling to the ACF buses prior to World War II but carried the Brill name. After the war, the ACF-Brill name was adopted for both trolley buses and buses built in the ACF plant. The first post-war trolley buses were similar to previous models but had a small windshield. A larger windshield was later featured as on the ACF-Brill Model TC-44, 10 of which were purchased in 1948 by the St. Joseph Light, Heat & Power Company in Missouri.

In 1948, Chicago Transit Authority acquired 120 Model T-44 ACF-Brill trolley buses. They were the latest design and were similar to the C-45 ACF-Brill motor buses, which had Westinghouse electrical equipment. Chicago also had one other ACF-Brill trolley bus, a Model TC-48. ACF-Brill built 927 trolley buses between 1945 and 1952. Chicago had the largest trolley bus fleet in the United States and operated 679 at its peak.

CCF-Brill IC-41 Intercity Buses

Saskatchewan Transportation Company was established April 1, 1946, by the Saskatchewan government, resulting in public ownership of intercity bus service in the province. However, after some debate, the provincial routes of Western Canadian Greyhound Lines were allowed. To operate the provincial routes acquired, Saskatchewan Transportation Company took delivery of 38 buses, 18 of which were the CCF-Brill Model IC-37 (one pictured here). They were built in CCF-Brill's plant in Fort William, Ontario in 1946.

Gray Coach Company of Toronto was a good customer for CCF-Brill and CanCar buses, with 25 of these Model IC-41 coaches delivered in 1946. Gray Coach also had 55 Model C-36 CCF-Brill buses and 65 Model IUC-35 CCF-Brill buses. Gray Coach, incorporated on June 28, 1927, was a subsidiary of the Toronto Transportation Commission. It was sold to Greyhound Canada in 1992.

CCF-Brill Voyageur Intercity Buses

Canadian Car-Brill attempted to enter the small intercity coach market in the early 1950s. The result was the Model ICW-29 Voyageur, which was almost identical in appearance to the Flxible Clipper. An AEC 470-cubic-inch inline 6-cylinder diesel engine was used. Beaver Bus Line of Winnipeg, Manitoba, had this 1952 Voyageur and used it on its Winnipeg-Selkirk, Manitoba, service.

Canada Coach Lines of Hamilton, Ontario, bought 20 of the 37 Canadian Car-Brill Voyageur Model ICW-29 intercity coaches; one is pictured here. Even though only 37 were built, production continued from 1950 through 1955. The Voyageur had seating for 29 passengers, along with sizable baggage storage at the rear. Canada Coach Lines was a subsidiary of the Hamilton Street Railway Company and operated a number of routes in Southern Ontario.

CCF-Brill Model IUC-35 Bus

International Transit Limited of Port Arthur (also known as Thunder Bay North), Ontario, acquired this Model IUC-35 CCF-Brill bus in 1947. It was a suburban or interurban version of the Model C-36. International Transit was the only company in addition to Toronto's Gray Coach Co. and Montreal's Provincial Transport Co. that had this model. Only 113 units were built. International Transit also had two Model IC-41 CCF-Brill intercity coaches.

CCF-Brill Model C-36 City Buses

London Street Railway Company in Ontario was one of the first Canadian companies to purchase the C-36 CCF-Brill bus. In 1945, 35 were acquired, then another 15 the following year, and 17 more in 1947. Shown here is one of the first Model C-36 buses delivered to London. These buses had Hall-Scott underfloor 477-cubic-inch gasoline engines. More than 1,000 Model C-36 CCF-Brill buses were built.

Sudbury Transit in Ontario bought two CCF-Brill (CanCar) Model C-36 ATC buses (one pictured here) in 1950. The Model C-36 ATC had an underfloor AEC 6-cylinder diesel engine with a torque converter. In 1950, CanCar recognized that diesel engines were becoming favored by bus operators and offered the AEC diesel engine as an option. A steel frame for the bus was also new in 1950. Forty-three Model C-36A buses were built.

CCF-Brill Model C-44A City Bus

The Toronto Transit Commission had a variety of bus makes, including a number of CCF-Brill (CanCar) buses, in its fleet. Pictured here is one of five CanCar Model CD-44A buses purchased in 1956. These buses had roof windows and were used in sightseeing and other special services in the Toronto area. This model had a front vent over the destination sign, and had an AEC 6-cylinder diesel engine mounted under the floor.

CCF-Brill Model C-52 City

The Montreal Transportation Commission succeeded Montreal Tramways Company in 1951. Buses, including those running on the busy St. Catherine's Street route, were replacing most of Montreal's streetcars. This Can-Car Model CD-52TC was in a group of 50 added in 1956 along with 50 Mack buses to replace the St. Catherine's Street streetcars. The Model CD-52TC was the largest bus built by CanCar at the time, and had AEC horizontal diesel engines.

CCF-Brill Trolley Buses

Vancouver's British Columbia Electric Company began operating trolley buses in 1948. The first group of trolley buses was 82 CCF-Brill Model TC-44 units. More TC-44, T-48s, and T-48A Models were added later. When this picture was taken, this CCF-Brill T-44 was operated by BC Hydro, the successor to the British Columbia Electric Company. Vancouver had the largest Canadian fleet of trolley buses, 327 at its peak. All the Vancouver orders accounted for one-third of CCF-Brill's trolley bus production.

One of the 16 Canadian cities that operated CCF-Brill trolley buses was Hamilton, Ontario. The Hamilton Street Railway Company began in 1875. It had 48 CCF-Brill Model T-48 and T-48A trolley buses. Hamilton began operating trolley buses in 1950 and ended in 1992. When the service began, 18 trolley buses were received and 30 Model T-348A CCF-Brill trolley buses (one pictured here) were delivered in 1950.

CanCar Model T-43 and T-52 City Buses

CCF-Brill became CanCar in 1956. The company introduced the newly designed Models TD-43 and TD-51 transit buses in 1960. The prototype TD-51 bus is shown here. These models had an AEC A690 diesel engine mounted transversely in the rear. Eight Canadian properties bought the Model TD-51 buses and five bought the Model TD-43. The buses were introduced at a time when General Motors began building buses in Canada and became a serious competitor. Only 200 of these two models were built; the last was delivered in 1962.

The CanCar TD-51 and TD-43 Models were introduced in 1960. Regina Transit System in Saskatchewan had 6 of the 26 TD-43 Models that were built. This model had a rear-mounted, 175-horsepower AEC-A 690 diesel engine. Regina Transit also had 16 Model C-36 CCF-Brill buses, and had purchased 55 CCF-Brill Model T-44 and T-48 trolley buses, although 17 were lost in a car barn fire soon after delivery.

107

Manitoba's Greater Winnipeg Transit System had been a good CCF-Brill and CanCar customer for a number of years. When the new Model TD-51 CanCar bus was introduced in 1960, Greater Winnipeg purchased 25 of the new 51-passenger buses, one of which is pictured here on Portage Avenue. An AEC diesel engine was mounted in the rear. The Model TD-51 and companion Model TD-43 were manufactured in the CanCar plant in Montreal. Production of the two models ended in 1963.

CCF-Brill Exported Buses

In 1948, CCF-Brill received an order for 113 Model IC-41 highway coaches from South African Railways. Pictured here are postcard views of the CCF-Brill Model IC-41 coaches, published by South African Railways.

109

ACF and ACF-Brill Customer Time Tables

Massachusetts and New York bus companies promoted ACF and ACF-Brill buses on their timetable covers.

Blue Ridge Lines, Boston & Maine Transportation, and Saskatchewan Transportation Co. displayed their ACF and ACF-Brills on their timetable covers.

111

National Trailways Bus System members presented ACF-Brill buses on their timetable covers.

Continental Trailways used pictures of ACF-Brill buses on various brochures promoting tours and travel.

113

ACF and ACF-Brill Sales Literature

Here is an unusual "small capacity" coach — Every single part and unit has been designed expressly for bus service! A TRUE BUS!

a. c. f.

This Model 85 ACF small bus was promoted with this brochure in 1930.

This 1936 sales brochure promoted the ACF Model H-9-P intercity buses, which were receiving many repeat orders.

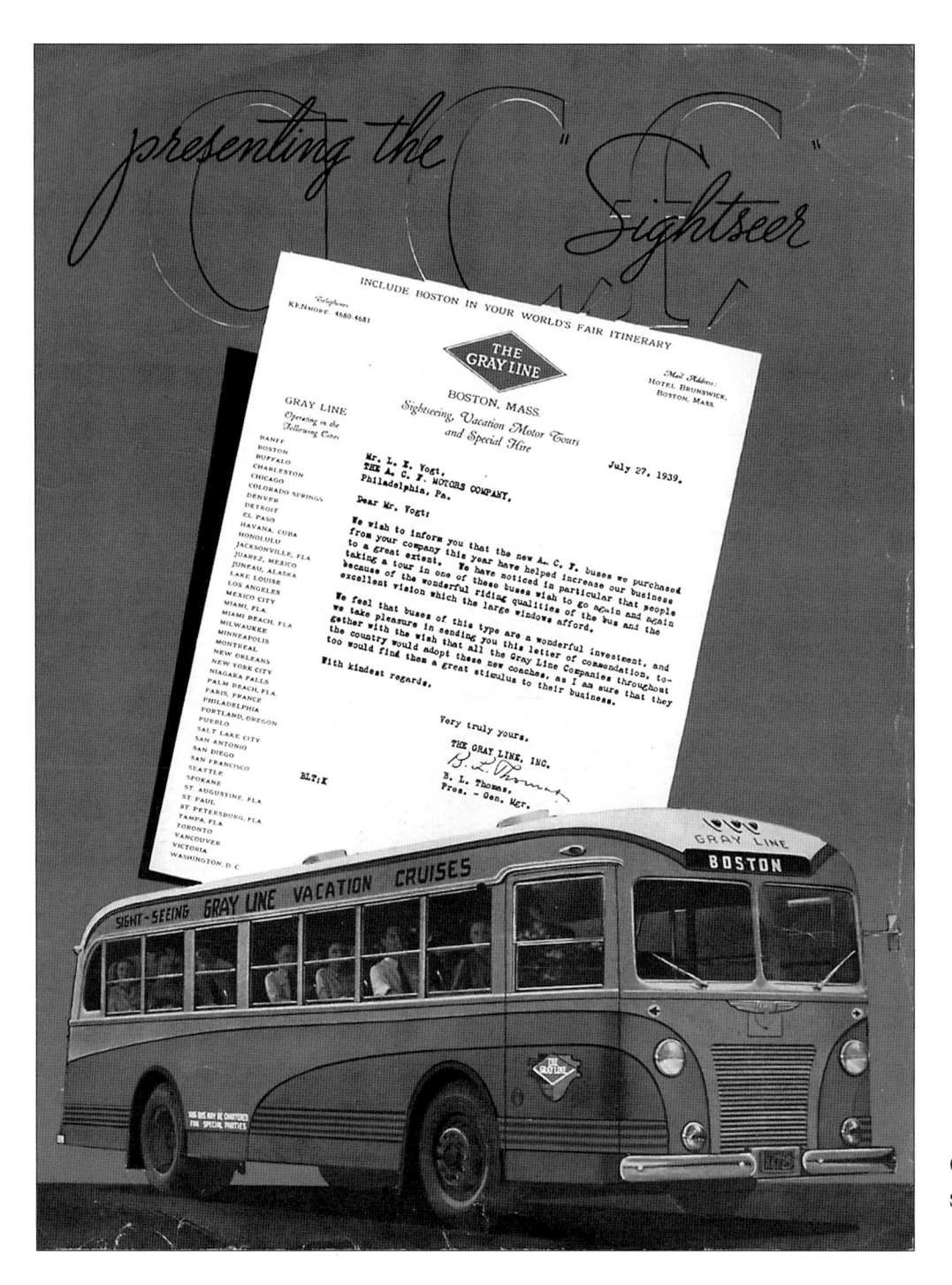

Gray Line of Boston liked the new ACF sightseeing buses, as noted in this sales leaflet of 1939.

116

This six-panel brochure promoted the new 29-passenger ACF intercity bus in 1939.

Two Big Shots
FOR DEFENSE TRAFFIC

At this opportune moment **a.C.f.** introduces two new and improved large-capacity coaches which will enable many transit companies to operate busy lines with greater efficiency, reliability, and economy.

Like other **a.C.f.** models, the new 41-S and 45-S models are Underfloor Powered because of the greater total capacity, the fuel-conserving Straight Line Drive, the reliable Hall-Scott horizontal engine — the ease and accessibility for Low-Cost Maintenance, and the Low Center of Gravity, increased Stability and Smooth Riding.

Such experienced **a.C.f.** operators as Eastern Massachusetts Street Railway of Boston, United Electric Railways of Providence, Worcester Street Railway, Aronimink Transportation Company, Fort Worth Transit Company, Boston Elevated Railway, and others have already placed orders for substantial quantities of these new models including models equipped with either Fluidgear or conventional Syncromesh transmissions.

At the time of World War II, ACF presented this advertisement for its Model 41-S and 45-S buses.

The U.S. Navy bought 35 ACF Model 41-S buses in 1941–1942, as ACF proudly proclaimed in this sales piece.

The new ACF-Brill Model C-36 was presented in this sales brochure from January 1946.

Hall-Scott Engines, a part of ACF-Brill, were promoted in this 1948 brochure.

LET'S LOOK UP for "CENTS power"

..true economy with

HALL-SCOTT ENGINES

exclusively in

ACF-BRILL COACHES

INTERCITY TRANSIT

121

The small Brill Models C-31 and C-27, introduced in 1948, received publicity with this sales folder.

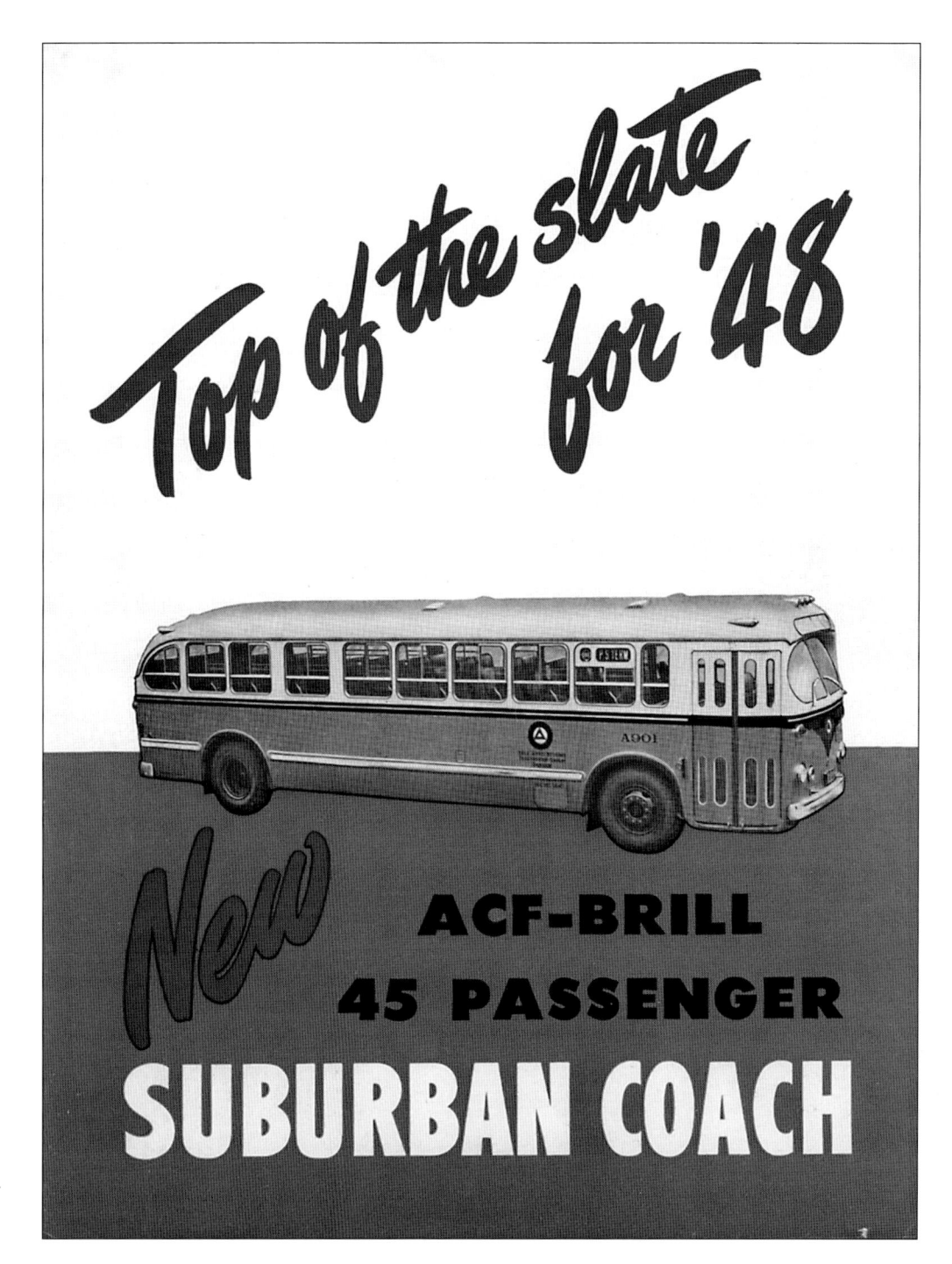

The Suburban ACF-Brill Model C-45 was advertised with this full-color piece in 1948.

Southeastern Greyhound Lines was featured in this 1947 ACF sales brochure.

Hats off!

to the *New*

CONTINENTAL BUS SYSTEM

and to its

new **ACF-BRILL COACHES**

With schedules covering over 20,000 miles of routes, the new Continental Bus System is today one of the world's largest integrated bus operations. Shown here is one of the *59 new ACF-Brill Coaches* now being delivered to Continental. These new buses will be added to a fleet of 590 ACF-Brill coaches purchased during the past 13 years by the various properties now included in the new system.

Continental Bus System was given "Hats Off" with the sales brochures presented in 1948.

125

About the Author

Buses began to fascinate me while I was in school in the 1930s. I began reading *Bus Transportation* magazine with great interest, and it was through the pages of that trade journal that I learned about ACF buses. The big ACF intercity buses caught my eye, and I was eager to see and ride them. Unfortunately, there were no ACF buses in the area of Minnesota where I lived at the time.

My first opportunity to see and ride an ACF bus was in the Chicago area in 1942. I was visiting Forest Park, a suburb of Chicago, and one evening, I rode my first ACF bus. It was a Chicago West Towns Railways Model 31-S ACF city bus. I also visited the Trailways bus terminal and saw the big ACF highway buses that were operated by Santa Fe Trailways, but there wasn't time to ride one.

The next year I found myself in the army, and eventually I had the opportunity to ride several ACF intercity buses. When I was stationed in Florida, I rode one of Florida Motor Lines' ACF Model 37-P buses. Later, while in Virginia, I rode Carolina Trailways ACF buses.

My interest in bus transportation persisted following my time in the army. I continued making model buses, carving them out of wood blocks and painting them in appropriate colors. Among my works were several ACF-Brill and CCF-Brill models. I wrote to ACF-Brill for pictures and specifications telling them that I was making models, and received very good information and photographs. In return, the ACF-Brill people asked me to send them a model. I made and sent two or three of the models especially for the ACF-Brill people.

In the summer of 1946, I had a very special experience: the opportunity to visit the CCF-Brill factory in Fort William (also known as Thunder Bay South), Ontario. There I saw CCF-Brill buses in production. It was the first bus factory I visited, although I have now visited more than 60 bus factories worldwide.

Bill Luke shows several of the ACF, ACF-Brill, and CCF-Brill model buses he made during the 1940s.

Later I traveled to the West Coast and rode a number of ACF and ACF-Brill intercity buses. These buses had a passenger seat immediately to the right of the driver, and the entrance door was behind that seat. It was very good for sightseeing as well as observing the driver who proudly and skillfully shifted the gears and maneuvered the big steering wheel. I occupied that special passenger seat over many of my travels. One of the special thrills was to ride the ACF-Brill buses of Rio Grande Trailways over the Canadian Rockies.

It was unfortunate that, like a number of other bus manufacturers after World War II, ACF-Brill discontinued bus manufacturing. Some ACF-Brill buses have been preserved; in particular, Greyhound has restored a Model IC-41 ACF-Brill that operated for Southeastern Greyhound Lines. Another Model IC-41 is being restored at the Greyhound Origin Bus Museum in Hibbing, Minnesota.

I have especially enjoyed producing this Photo Archive book about ACF and ACF-Brill buses and sharing the many interesting photographs in my collection as well as those of others' collections. Another bus history book I recently authored, *Bus Industry Chronicle*, has more photos of ACF, ACF-Brill, and CCF-Brill buses and historical information about those companies.

I have also had the opportunity to record additional bus industry history in several other photo-archive volumes: *Greyhound Buses 1914–2000 Photo Archive*, *Trailways Buses 1936–2001 Photo Archive*, *Buses of Motor Coach Industries 1932–2000 Photo Archive*, *Yellow Coach Buses 1923–1943 Photo Archive*, *Trolley Buses 1913–2001 Photo Archive*, *Fageol & Twin Coach Buses 1922–1956 Photo Archive*, and *Prevost Buses 1924–2002 Photo Archive*.

AMERICAN CULTURE

Coca-Cola: A History in Photographs 1930-1969 ISBN 1-882256-46-8
Coca-Cola: Its Vehicles in Photographs 1930-1969 ISBN 1-882256-47-6
Phillips 66 1945-1954 Photo Archive ISBN 1-882256-42-5

AUTOMOTIVE

AMX Photo Archive: From Concept to Reality ISBN 1-58388-062-3
Auburn Automobiles 1900-1936 Photo Archive ISBN 1-58388-093-3
Camaro 1967-2000 Photo Archive ISBN 1-58388-032-1
Checker Cab Co. Photo History ISBN 1-58388-100-X
Chevrolet Station Wagons 1946-1966 Photo Archive ISBN 1-58388-069-0
Classic American Limousines 1955-2000 Photo Archive ISBN 1-58388-041-0
Corvair by Chevrolet Experimental & Production Cars 1957-1969, Ludvigsen Library Series ISBN 1-58388-058-5
Corvette The Exotic Experimental Cars, Ludvigsen Library Series ISBN 1-58388-017-8
Corvette Prototypes & Show Cars Photo Album ISBN 1-882256-77-8
Early Ford V-8s 1932-1942 Photo Album ISBN 1-882256-97-2
Ferrari- The Factory Maranello's Secrets 1950-1975, Ludvigsen Library Series ISBN 1-58388-085-2
Ford Postwar Flatheads 1946-1953 Photo Archive ISBN 1-58388-080-1
Ford Station Wagons 1929-1991 Photo History ISBN 1-58388-103-4
Imperial 1955-1963 Photo Archive ISBN 1-882256-22-0
Imperial 1964-1968 Photo Archive ISBN 1-882256-23-9
Javelin Photo Archive: From Concept to Reality ISBN 1-58388-071-2
Lincoln Motor Cars 1920-1942 Photo Archive ISBN 1-882256-57-3
Lincoln Motor Cars 1946-1960 Photo Archive ISBN 1-882256-58-1
Nash 1936-1957 Photo Archive ISBN 1-58388-086-0
Packard Motor Cars 1935-1942 Photo Archive ISBN 1-882256-44-1
Packard Motor Cars 1946-1958 Photo Archive ISBN 1-882256-45-X
Pontiac Dream Cars, Show Cars & Prototypes 1928-1998 Photo Album ISBN 1-882256-93-X
Pontiac Firebird Trans-Am 1969-1999 Photo Album ISBN 1-882256-95-6
Pontiac Firebird 1967-2000 Photo History ISBN 1-58388-028-3
Rambler 1950-1969 Photo Archive ISBN 1-58388-078-X
Stretch Limousines 1928-2001 Photo Archive ISBN 1-58388-070-4
Studebaker 1933-1942 Photo Archive ISBN 1-882256-24-7
Studebaker Hawk 1956-1964 Photo Archive ISBN 1-58388-094-1
Studebaker Lark 1959-1966 Photo Archive ISBN 1-58388-107-7
Ultimate Corvette Trivia Challenge ISBN 1-58388-035-6

BUSES

Buses of ACF Photo Archive ISBN 1-58388-101-8
Buses of Motor Coach Industries 1932-2000 Photo Archive ISBN 1-58388-039-9
Fageol & Twin Coach Buses 1922-1956 Photo Archive ISBN 1-58388-075-5
Flxible Intercity Buses 1924-1970 Photo Archive ISBN 1-58388-108-5
Flxible Transit Buses 1953-1995 Photo Archive ISBN 1-58388-053-4
GM Intercity Coaches 1944-1980 Photo Archive ISBN 1-58388-099-2
Greyhound Buses 1914-2000 Photo Archive ISBN 1-58388-027-5
*Mack® Buses 1900-1960 Photo Archive** ISBN 1-58388-020-8
Prevost Buses 1924-2002 Photo Archive ISBN 1-58388-083-6
Trailways Buses 1936-2001 Photo Archive ISBN 1-58388-029-1
Trolley Buses 1913-2001 Photo Archive ISBN 1-58388-057-7
Yellow Coach Buses 1923-1943 Photo Archive ISBN 1-58388-054-2

EMERGENCY VEHICLES

The American Ambulance 1900-2002: An Illustrated History ISBN 1-58388-081-X
American Funeral Vehicles 1883-2003 Illustrated History ISBN 1-58388-104-2
American LaFrance 700 Series 1945-1952 Photo Archive ISBN 1-882256-90-5
American LaFrance 700 Series 1945-1952 Photo Archive Volume 2 ISBN 1-58388-025-9
American LaFrance 700 & 800 Series 1953-1958 Photo Archive ISBN 1-882256-91-3
American LaFrance 900 Series 1958-1964 Photo Archive ISBN 1-58388-002-X
Classic Seagrave 1935-1951 Photo Archive ISBN 1-58388-034-8
Crown Firecoach 1951-1985 Photo Archive ISBN 1-58388-047-X
Fire Chief Cars 1900-1997 Photo Album ISBN 1-882256-87-5
Hahn Fire Apparatus 1923-1990 Photo Archive ISBN 1-58388-077-1
Heavy Rescue Trucks 1931-2000 Photo Gallery ISBN 1-58388-045-3
Imperial Fire Apparatus 1969-1976 Photo Archive ISBN 1-58388-091-7
Industrial and Private Fire Apparatus 1925-2001 Photo Archive ISBN 1-58388-049-6
Los Angeles City Fire Apparatus 1953-1999 Photo Archive ISBN 1-58388-012-7
*Mack Model C Fire Trucks 1957-1967 Photo Archive** ISBN 1-58388-014-3
*Mack Model L Fire Trucks 1940-1954 Photo Archive** ISBN 1-882256-86-7
Maxim Fire Apparatus 1914-1989 Photo Archive ISBN 1-58388-050-X
Navy & Marine Corps Fire Apparatus 1836 -2000 Photo Gallery ISBN 1-58388-031-3
Pierre Thibault Ltd. Fire Apparatus 1918-1990 Photo Archive ISBN 1-58388-074-7
Pirsch Fire Apparatus 1890-1991 Photo Archive ISBN 1-58388-082-8
Police Cars: Restoring, Collecting & Showing America's Finest Sedans ISBN 1-58388-046-1
Saulsbury Fire Rescue Apparatus 1956-2003 Photo Archive ISBN 1-58388-106-9
Seagrave 70th Anniversary Series Photo Archive ISBN 1-58388-001-1
TASC Fire Apparatus 1946-1985 Photo Archive ISBN 1-58388-065-8
Volunteer & Rural Fire Apparatus Photo Gallery ISBN 1-58388-005-4
W.S. Darley & Co. Fire Apparatus 1908-2000 Photo Archive ISBN 1-58388-061-5
Ward LaFrance Fire Trucks 1918-1978 Photo Archive ISBN 1-58388-013-5
Wildland Fire Apparatus 1940-2001 Photo Gallery ISBN 1-58388-056-9
Young Fire Equipment 1932-1991 Photo Archive ISBN 1-58388-015-1

RACING

Chaparral Can-Am Racing Cars from Texas, Ludvigsen Library Series ISBN 1-58388-066-6
Cunningham Sports Cars, Ludvigsen Library Series ISBN 1-58388-109-3
Drag Racing Funny Cars of the 1960s Photo Archive ISBN 1-58388-097-6
Drag Racing Funny Cars of the 1970s Photo Archive ISBN 1-58388-068-2
El Mirage Impressions: Dry Lakes Land Speed Racing ISBN 1-58388-059-3
GT40 Photo Archive ISBN 1-882256-64-6
Indy Cars of the 1950s, Ludvigsen Library Series ISBN 1-58388-018-6
Indy Cars of the 1960s, Ludvigsen Library Series ISBN 1-58388-052-6
Indy Cars of the 1970s, Ludvigsen Library Series ISBN 1-58388-098-4
Indianapolis Racing Cars of Frank Kurtis 1941-1963 Photo Archive ISBN 1-58388-026-7
Juan Manuel Fangio World Champion Driver Series Photo Album ISBN 1-58388-008-9

More Great Titles From Iconografix

All Iconografix books are available from direct mail specialty book dealers and bookstores worldwide, or can be ordered from the publisher. For book trade and distribution information or to add your name to our mailing list and receive a **FREE CATALOG** contact:

Iconografix,
PO Box 446, Dept BK
Hudson, WI, 54016

Telephone: (715) 381-9755,
(800) 289-3504 (USA),
Fax: (715) 381-9756

*This product is sold under license from Mack Trucks, Inc. Mack is a registered Trademark of Mack Trucks, Inc. All rights reserved.

Lost Race Tracks Treasures of Automobile Racing ISBN 1-58388-084-4
Mario Andretti World Champion Driver Series Photo Album ISBN 1-58388-009-7
Mercedes-Benz 300SL Racing Cars 1952-1953, Ludvigsen Library Series ISBN 1-58388-067-4
Novi V-8 Indy Cars 1941-1965, Ludvigsen Library Series ISBN 1-58388-037-2
Porsche Spyders Type 550 1953-1956, Ludvigsen Library Series ISBN 1-58388-092-5
Sebring 12-Hour Race 1970 Photo Archive ISBN 1-882256-20-4
Vanderbilt Cup Race 1936 & 1937 Photo Archive ISBN 1-882256-66-2

RAILWAYS

Chicago, St. Paul, Minneapolis & Omaha Railway 1880-1940 Photo Archive ISBN 1-882256-67-0
Chicago & North Western Railway 1975-1995 Photo Archive ISBN 1-882256-76-X
Great Northern Railway 1945-1970 Volume 2 Photo Archive ISBN 1-882256-79-4
Great Northern Railway Ore Docks of Lake Superior Photo Archive ISBN 1-58388-073-9
Illinois Central Railroad 1854-1960 Photo Archive ISBN 1-58388-063-1
Milwaukee Road 1850-1960 Photo Archive ISBN 1-882256-61-1
Milwaukee Road Depots 1856-1954 Photo Archive ISBN 1-58388-040-2
Show Trains of the 20th Century ISBN 1-58388-030-5
Soo Line 1975-1992 Photo Archive ISBN 1-882256-68-9
Steam Locomotives of the B&O Railroad Photo Archive ISBN 1-58388-095-X
Streamliners to the Twin Cities Photo Archive 400, Twin Zephyrs & Hiawatha Trains ISBN 1-58388-096-8
Trains of the Twin Ports Photo Archive, Duluth-Superior in the 1950s ISBN 1-58388-003-8
Trains of the Circus 1872-1956 ISBN 1-58388-024-0
Trains of the Upper Midwest Photo Archive Steam & Diesel in the 1950s & 1960s ISBN 1-58388-036-4
Wisconsin Central Limited 1987-1996 Photo Archive ISBN 1-882256-75-1
Wisconsin Central Railway 1871-1909 Photo Archive ISBN 1-882256-78-6

RECREATIONAL VEHICLES

Ski-Doo Racing Sleds 1960-2003 Photo Archive ISBN 1-58388-105-0

TRUCKS

Autocar Trucks 1950-1987 Photo Archive ISBN 1-58388-072-0
Beverage Trucks 1910-1975 Photo Archive ISBN 1-882256-60-3
*Brockway Trucks 1948-1961 Photo Archive** ISBN 1-882256-55-7
Chevrolet El Camino Photo History Incl. GMC Sprint & Caballero ISBN 1-58388-044-5
Circus and Carnival Trucks 1923-2000 Photo Archive ISBN 1-58388-048-8
Dodge B-Series Trucks Restorer's & Collector's Reference Guide and History ISBN 1-58388-087-9
Dodge Pickups 1939-1978 Photo Album ISBN 1-882256-82-4
Dodge Power Wagons 1940-1980 Photo Archive ISBN 1-882256-89-1
Dodge Power Wagon Photo History ISBN 1-58388-019-4
Dodge Ram Trucks 1994-2001 Photo History ISBN 1-58388-051-8
Dodge Trucks 1929-1947 Photo Archive ISBN 1-882256-36-0
Dodge Trucks 1948-1960 Photo Archive ISBN 1-882256-37-9
Ford 4x4s 1935-1990 Photo History ISBN 1-58388-079-8
Ford Heavy-Duty Trucks 1948-1998 Photo History ISBN 1-58388-043-7
Freightliner Trucks 1937-1981 Photo Archive ISBN 1-58388-090-9
Jeep 1941-2000 Photo Archive ISBN 1-58388-021-6
Jeep Prototypes & Concept Vehicles Photo Archive ISBN 1-58388-033-X
*Mack Model AB Photo Archive** ISBN 1-882256-18-2
*Mack AP Super-Duty Trucks 1926-1938 Photo Archive** ISBN 1-882256-54-9
*Mack Model B 1953-1966 Volume 2 Photo Archive** ISBN 1-882256-34-4
*Mack EB-EC-ED-EE-EF-EG-DE 1936-1951 Photo Archive** ISBN 1-882256-29-8
*Mack EH-EJ-EM-EQ-ER-ES 1936-1950 Photo Archive** ISBN 1-882256-39-5
*Mack FC-FCSW-NW 1936-1947 Photo Archive** ISBN 1-882256-28-X
*Mack FG-FH-FJ-FK-FN-FP-FT-FW 1937-1950 Photo Archive** ISBN 1-882256-35-2
*Mack LF-LH-LJ-LM-LT 1940-1956 Photo Archive** ISBN 1-882256-38-7
*Mack Trucks Photo Gallery** ISBN 1-882256-88-3
New Car Carriers 1910-1998 Photo Album ISBN 1-882256-98-0
Plymouth Commercial Vehicles Photo Archive ISBN 1-58388-004-6
Refuse Trucks Photo Archive ISBN 1-58388-042-9
RVs & Campers 1900-2000: An Illustrated History ISBN 1-58388-064-X
Studebaker Trucks 1927-1940 Photo Archive ISBN 1-882256-40-9
White Trucks 1900-1937 Photo Archive ISBN 1-882256-80-8

TRACTORS & CONSTRUCTION EQUIPMENT

Case Tractors 1912-1959 Photo Archive ISBN 1-882256-32-8
Caterpillar Photo Gallery ISBN 1-882256-70-0
Caterpillar Pocket Guide The Track-Type Tractors 1925-1957 ISBN 1-58388-022-4
Caterpillar D-2 & R-2 Photo Archive ISBN 1-882256-99-9
Caterpillar D-8 1933-1974 Photo Archive Incl. Diesel 75 & RD-8 ISBN 1-882256-96-4
Caterpillar Military Tractors Volume 1 Photo Archive ISBN 1-882256-16-6
Caterpillar Military Tractors Volume 2 Photo Archive ISBN 1-882256-17-4
Caterpillar Sixty Photo Archive ISBN 1-882256-05-0
Caterpillar Ten Photo Archive Incl. 7c Fifteen & High Fifteen ISBN 1-58388-011-9
Caterpillar Thirty Photo Archive 2ND Ed. Incl. Best Thirty, 6G Thirty & R-4 ISBN 1-58388-006-2
Circus & Carnival Tractors 1930-2001 Photo Archive ISBN 1-58388-076-3
Cletrac and Oliver Crawlers Photo Archive ISBN 1-882256-43-3
Classic American Steamrollers 1871-1935 Photo Archive ISBN 1-58388-038-0
Farmall Cub Photo Archive ISBN 1-882256-71-9
Farmall F-Series Photo Archive ISBN 1-882256-02-6
Farmall Model H Photo Archive ISBN 1-882256-03-4
Farmall Model M Photo Archive ISBN 1-882256-15-8
Farmall Regular Photo Archive ISBN 1-882256-14-X
Farmall Super Series Photo Archive ISBN 1-882256-49-2
Fordson 1917-1928 Photo Archive ISBN 1-882256-33-6
Hart-Parr Photo Archive ISBN 1-882256-08-5
Holt Tractors Photo Archive ISBN 1-882256-10-7
International TracTracTor Photo Archive ISBN 1-882256-48-4
John Deere Model A Photo Archive ISBN 1-882256-12-3
John Deere Model D Photo Archive ISBN 1-882256-00-X
Marion Construction Machinery 1884-1975 Photo Archive ISBN 1-58388-060-7
Marion Mining & Dredging Machines Photo Archive ISBN 1-58388-088-7
Oliver Tractors Photo Archive ISBN 1-882256-09-3
Russell Graders Photo Archive ISBN 1-882256-11-5
Twin City Tractor Photo Archive ISBN 1-882256-06-9

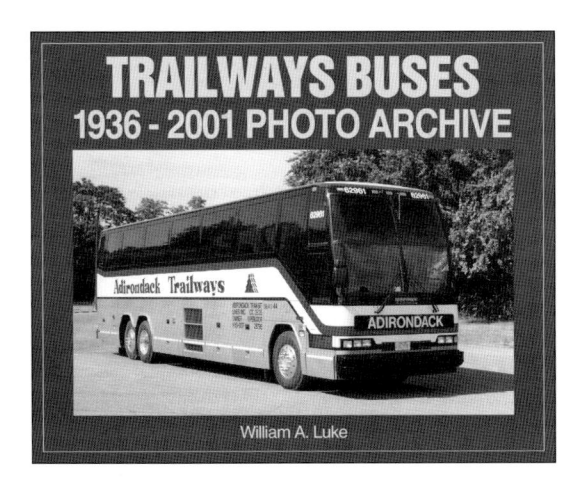

More great books from
Iconografix

Flxible Intercity Buses 1924-1970 Photo Archive
ISBN 1-58388-108-5

GM IntercityCoaches 1944-1980 Photo Archive
ISBN 1-58388-099-2

Prevost Buses 1924-2002 Photo Archive
ISBN 1-58388-083-6

Buses of Motor Coach Industries 1932-2000
Photo Archive   ISBN 1-58388-039-9

Trailways Buses 1936-2001 Photo Archive
ISBN 1-58388-029-1

Greyhound Buses 1914-2000 Photo Archive
ISBN 1-58388-027-5

Trolley Buses 1913-2001 Photo Archive
ISBN 1-58388-057-7

Iconografix, Inc.
P.O. Box 446, Dept BK,
Hudson, WI 54016
For a **free catalog** call: 1-800-289-3504

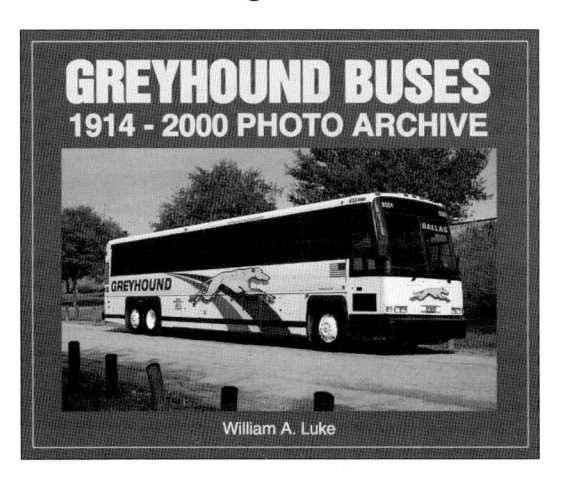

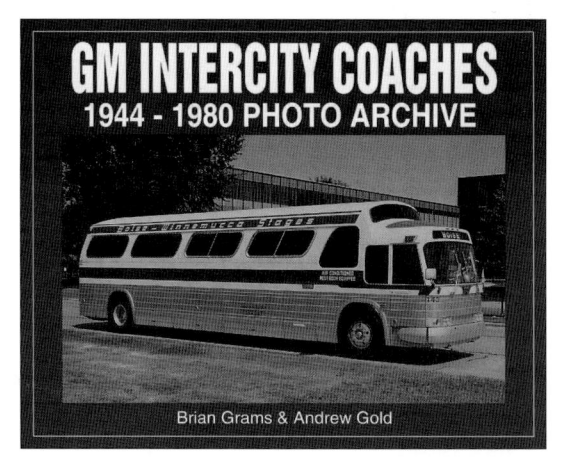

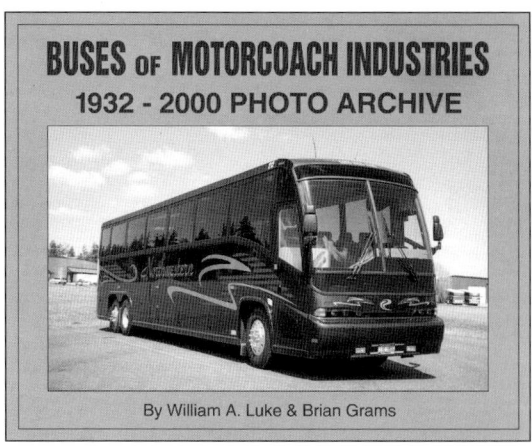

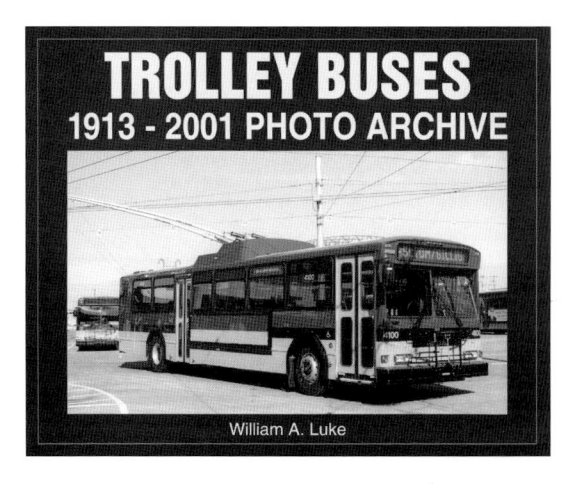